LAYERS

Volume I

I0212809

WHO AM I?

WHY AM I?

Authored By:

Empress Makeda N. Gordon

DEDICATION

A special Thank You to my mother, Dr. Cynthia Shannon, who is the strongest woman I know. Through every experience in my life, she has been my rock. Without her, I would not be half the woman I am today. Thank you from the depths of my heart Mommy! I love you.

ACKNOWLEGEMENTS

All Praise and Honor to my source, the Most High, Jah Rastafari. I am very grateful to H.I.M. for trusting me with every experience I have encountered. HE knew that I would take them and use them to do something Great.

Last, but never the least, my sisters, Alisia Pratt and Sabriya Wise. Stepping into womanhood was easy because of you. Both of you have been my anchor during the most challenging times in my life. I love you both dearly.

Table of Contents

About the Author

In June of 1977, a baby girl was born in Philadelphia, Pennsylvania. A completely innocent, void of all impurities, and ready for life, bouncing baby girl. Unbeknownst to her, or anyone else, life would allow her to experience so much pain, abuse, and trauma so early on. Each experience breaking through her innocence, destroying her confidence, her ability to reason, and so much more; all while building a woman of strength and virtue.

Makeda was born Nizaree Pratt. By age five, she had been exposed to a home filled with physical abuse. While she was not the direct victim of this abuse, she was affected by watching what she felt marriage was. At the age of nine, she had lost her sexual innocence, carrying on through the age of twelve years old. Age twelve opened a chapter of promiscuity. This was now her belief in her "purpose" here on earth; to be man's pleasure. By the age of thirteen, Niza found herself in what was her own first physically abusive relationship, which lasted until fifteen where she became pregnant with her abuser's child. This became a turning point in Niza's life; her son became her new purpose and was a new beginning for her.

Things seemingly began to look brighter; by age twenty, when Niza married a "God Fearing" man and was carrying her third child. At twenty-two years old she yielded the birth of her fourth and final child.

Marriage was apparently good, going through the motions without a clue of what was real and what was not. She became a chameleon to her husband and those she deemed "valuable", never taking a moment to learn about herself. Ten years later, the marriage ended and her life crumbled. She was now a single mother again with four times the children. Struggling to rebuild her life, she took on a toxic lifestyle filled with drugs, alcohol, and promiscuity. All of which was a failed attempt to numb the pain, find love and peace.

Now thirty-two years old, Niza decides to marry again. This time it was to a woman. I made myself believe that women love better, they understand better. Three months into the marriage, and eleven months into the relationship, she walked away due to serious physical abuse. Lost, confused, broken and exhausted, she ran into a man that exposed her to a path of redemption and purification from this toxic life she had claimed. This was a crucifixion, the ending of a life, painfully realized, and the purgation of Nizaree Pratt/West/Turlington!

For the next two years, she shut out television, radio, friends and family and went into self in an effort to find out who she truly was. She needed to Know and Overstand Who and Why she was. During that two-year period of time she met her "Pain Body" and saved herself from it. She found Faith, Standards, Morals, Values, and Peace.

The Pain Body is the part of us that is broken and/or damaged due to trauma in our lives. It is build and matures through our interactions, observances and experiences, from a very young age, and shapes Who and What we become, as well as how we view the world.

Spending all of her free time, outside of work, the children, studying the Bible, self-help books, and every piece of material she could get her hands on that would help her to grow and heal.

By age thirty-eight she was strong and had a sound mind; with a clear overstanding of who She was and Her Divine Purpose. Makeda was conceived right then and there, and Nizaree ceased to exist completely. Now knowing that the whole reason for all of her pain, and misfortune, was for that very moment.

This book was and is The Purpose that is now being realized. The edification of the sisters. During her search, she came across many women with the same story as hers. The only difference she saw was that they still had not identified their own Pain Bodies. They were still very much so, operating under the traumas of their own lives.

That is when She, I realized that it was time to write. Women, just like me, needed help. With all of the negativity that we have gotten from people for our "bad attitudes", "jealousies", "insecurities", and flat out "self-destructive" behaviors, we still have not been able to connect the dots. We still make decisions based on tainted information. And it is causing us to repeat a deadly cycle of dysfunction.

LAYERS Vol. 1 is written in Love, triggered by Pain and executed in Strength. My earnest prayer is that we evolve into the Queens that we were intended to be, since the very beginning of our creation.

No, I am no expert in the sense that society sees, which is through book knowledge and traditional degrees, however, I do consider myself an expert based on the merit of my experiences, as it IS the best teacher!

Therefore, My Sisters, I want to say thank you for taking this journey with me through this tool. And I pray that is blesses your life immensely.

Empress Makeda NaNa Gordon

Introduction

There comes a time in every woman's life, when she needs to take a step back and re-evaluate herself. She usually meets this time at a low point in her life. Maybe her heart was broken for the last time or maybe she is in the worst financial bind she has ever faced. It's possible that she has been feeling an overwhelming amount of discomfort within, due to her very own choices and/or actions. No matter what the circumstance is, LISTEN TO IT! Now is the time to make a change. The question is always, HOW?

My sister, as you read through this book and complete each exercise, honestly, and apply its lessons to your life moving forward, you will learn Love, Peace, and Happiness, like you never knew exist. And the best part is that it is not given by any external source, therefore it cannot be taken away by an external source. IT BELONGS TO YOU!

I believe that we all have Royalty lying within us, below the "Layers". If you don't believe me, take a look at your origin; study who you were Before slavery and oppression interrupted your history. Consider your Maker. There is a Queen living inside of us. It is up to us to find her, heal her and develop her into whomever we want her to be.

I employ you to not rush through this tool. Take your time, chapter by chapter. Give some real thought to your answers. Most of all my dear sister, BE HONEST with Self. The only way to make a lasting change of any kind, is to first acknowledge the problem(s). Then, and only then, can a solution be sought out.

(Please note: I am not a Psychologist/Psychiatrist or Licensed Therapist. The content of this book is based on life experience and spiritual guidance. In no way should this book be used in place of psychological expertise.)

Self-Evaluation Test

Let's take a "before" look. Fill in the answers to the best of your ability. This test is just an overview to give us a starting point on Self-Acknowledgement. Some of us have never even taken the time to think about some of these questions. I would like for you to review them after completing this book and see if any of your answers have changed.

All about you:

What is the meaning of your first name _____

Favorite Color _____

Favorite Food _____

Spiritual Faith _____

Was this faith chosen or taught _____

What is your basic belief on Spirituality/Religion and how did you come to that conclusion

_____

_____

_____

_____

What age were you when you lost your virginity ____

How many partners since then ____

Parenting:

How old were you when you had your first child _____

How many children do you have _____

How would you rate your parenting skills on a scale of 1-10

1 2 3 4 5 6 7 8 9 10

(Need help)   (I try)   (Award winning)

How do others rate your parenting skills on a scale of 1-10

1 2 3 4 5 6 7 8 9 10

(Lots of complaints)   (No feedback)   (Award winning)

Love:

Are you or have you been married (circle one) YES/NO

If YES, how many times _____

If NO, why do you think that is

_____

_____

_____

Would you say you fall in love quickly (circle one) YES/NO

How would you define love in your experience

_____

_____

_____

_____

_____

_____

What are your views on the role of a wife, in the home, in terms of duties?

_____

_____

_____

_____

What are your views on the role of the husband, in the home, in terms of duties?

_____

_____

_____

_____

Do you feel that your emotional, sexual, financial, and spiritual needs are being met in your current or last long-term relationship? (circle one) YES/NO

If NO, please explain why not

_____

_____

_____

_____

_____

_____

Have you ever suffered any type of abuse (physical, sexual, emotional, etc.) (Circle one) YES/NO

If yes, write out what happened, by who, and your thoughts about how it may be affecting your life today on the blank sheet of paper at the end of this evaluation.

Financial:

Do you consider yourself to be a good money manager (circle one) YES/NO

Why_____
_____
_____
_____

Do you currently have a least 3 months of bills in an emergency account (circle one) YES/NO

Do you currently have a retirement plan in place (circle one) YES/NO

Do you currently have a living Will (circle one) YES/NO

Do you pay your monthly bills on time? (circle one) YES/NO

Do you know your current FICA score? (circle one) YES/NO

Do you know your husband/significant other's FICA score? (circle one) YES/NO

Do you have some type of education fund set up for your children? (circle one) YES/NO

NOTES:

*What type of abuse?

*By who and what age

_____

*Possible effects on life today

_____

Foreword

One of the hardest questions to ever ask yourself is "Who Am I". The possible answer can be so terrifying. Giving thought to our shortcomings, or pain, can be a very difficult task. Most women are very comfortable hiding behind their beautiful curves and precisely painted faces. Isn't life so much easier that way?

Moving forward, we will cover a lot of ground on many topics in an effort to find Our Truth. This would be a great place to grab a notebook and pen, if you haven't already!

How many of us can wake up in the morning, walk straight over to your full-length mirror, stark naked, and say, I LOVE WHAT I SEE RIGHT NOW? Very few, I can tell you. Most of us have a daily routine based on the things we are most uncomfortable with. For instance, the woman who doesn't like her skin may put on make-up, or maybe it is your stomach that you feel is out of shape and so you wear a girdle of sorts. No matter what our "thing" is, we allot a little extra time, when getting ready, to make the necessary adjustments. These are the masks that Women wear Daily. Physical appearance is just a fraction of one of our many layers.

We are made up of three basic parts, Flesh, Spirit, and Soul. Now in order to have a full overstanding of what part each of these Layers play in our daily lives, we must first understand each one. Having the ability to identify your Personal Layers is a major accomplishment. Be sure to take your time and think deeply about your Triune Being. It is vast and detailed, but definitely abled to be known and understood. We have to find the connecting points of each basic part. For all three components must work in harmony in order for us to have a balanced life. We must know every part of ourselves before we can bring ourselves into alignment. Without Alignment we are never truly grounded.

Full Alignment is when your Mind/Intuition (Spirit), Heart (Soul), and Body (Flesh) are in agreement. One should never make any decisions except the three agree. That is the sure-fire recipe for regrets.

An example of this "dis-alignment" and how it can affect our lives would be; Meeting a man that you are physically (flesh) attracted to. As you spend time with him you begin to fall hard for him (heart), but this man has a reputation for being violent toward women. Your mind (spirit) is telling you that dating him is a bad idea. But you don't listen. So as time goes on you start to see his anger with others, but still not you. Still it raises "red flags" for you. However, you decide to rationalize by telling yourself "Well he is not like that with me". Then the day finally comes when her hits You. And as you nurse your wounds, you think to yourself that you should have listened. But now it is too late to turn back the hands of time; you have given yourself one more reason to hold on to the anger or bitterness. Simply because you chose not to listen to the reasoning of your Mind.

Fundamental Layer

"OUR TRIUNE BEING"

Third Dimension
(Thoughts & Feelings)

Our flesh is our "Expressed Being", is our Third Dimensional Being. It embodies our Physical Attributes such as our psyche, race, complexion, body type, how we think and our belief systems.

Our Physical Attributes, all but race, can be altered through many resources available in the world today. Make-up, cosmetic surgeries, tattooing and piercings, clothing, and exercising are just a few of them. However, our psyche is a whole different challenge. We are programmed to think and believe a certain way from the womb.

Those feelings began with the energy our mothers carried while we were yet inside. Then the words we heard spoken by her and around her (words of peace and love or pain and dysfunction) begins to mold our minds and speech. Once we were birthed into this 3D realm, we became susceptible to what we were exposed to. That exposure leads us to view our Physical Appearance in a certain, sometimes delusional way, and affects our Psyche in the way in which we think and feel about ourselves. The totality of these parts makes up our Self-Esteem and Self-Image, Self-Worth and fuels our future actions and behaviors.

How does one develop a positive or negative Self-Esteem/Self-Image through Physical Appearance? It is done through the likes and dislikes of the world around us. In other words, it is obtained through the things that we accept or those things that we reject. Now all things have a beginning, or origin, if you will, and this positive or negative Self-Esteem/Self-Image starts way before we are born. Our Subconscious minds from fetus to childhood, is like a sponge. It absorbs everything. And before we reach a certain age, we are defenseless to how to appropriate that information that is being uploaded into us through our environment.

It is very important that a pregnant woman is mindful of her thoughts and feelings while carrying her child. Remembering that we are that child's life source, that child's very existence is predicated on what they draw from the mother. Many take this to mean in the physical sense only, but they would be wrong. That baby is getting all of its nutrients and energy from us. However, their Soul is with them in the embryotic stage absorbing as well. It can only absorb what is provided for it. This, in most cases is the origin of the rejection issues many of us face. Although our little brains are not fully developed, our souls have a very proficient memory chip. So whatever is uploaded into us in the fetal stage will become what is downloaded into us after birth.

For example, if a Mother-to-be has consistent feelings of regret and/or remorse for her pregnancy, the infant feels that rejection and most times, according to studies, those are generally the children who are very uneasy as infants and have attachment and/or abandonment issues. It can sometimes cause the baby to not bond with the mother at all initially, or to "over-bond", meaning, it won't allow mom to move an inch away from them for a second without a major tantrum. Be it joyous and excited, or anger and regret, that baby will feel the love or rejection immediately, and it will grow with them the longer mom has those feelings.

The disgruntled mother doesn't usually invest the time and care it takes to create a loving environment for her child. She may not read, sing, or even talk to the baby. She may eat unhealthy foods or wear clothing that is not conducive to proper circulation for the infant, or ingest things that are harmful to the baby; like smoking, drinking or doing drugs. Whereas, the mother that is excited for her child, will attend every doctor visit, rub her belly, talk to her child, and begin mothering it before the birth has even taken place; giving the baby a loving and healthy environment in which to develop.

Point being, our feelings, thoughts, and emotions affect our little creations. The good news is that at any point, during your pregnancy, you can transmute that energy and change the trajectory of emotion you offer your child. So you see, the energy that our mothers carried us in, was the beginning of Self-Esteem for us.

Think back to your earliest memories, were your parents affectionate with you, did they tell you and show you they loved you often; or did they criticize everything you tried to do? Did they make fun of your short comings or physical attributes that were out of your control; such as weight, complexion, etc.? Being called fat, stupid or ugly vs beautiful, smart and a powerful can affect a child for many years to come. These statements cut us deeply both consciously and subconsciously. They most definitely follow that child throughout adulthood, if the behavior is not corrected and the emotional damage dealt with. In some cases we have to selfheal and accept the apology that is never given.

Here is another example on how origin affects us later in life.

If your household was one that prayed or meditated together daily or often, you, even as a child, will begin to see this practice as what families "do", as what you should do. Likewise, if you witnessed verbal vulgarity growing up, chances are that some of your first words will be those very same vulgarities. The molding has begun. Children often follow their parents Actions more than their Verbal Instructions. So when a parent does not exhibit the evidence of the teachings they give, it plants a seed of distrust in a child. And once a child is no longer able to trust their parent, it is exceedingly difficult to get them to accept your parenting as something beneficial to them. This is where you begin to see the child "act out" with misbehavior.

As we grow older, we begin to have more understanding of our surroundings, we soak it all in consciously and subconsciously, be it positive or negative. A foundation of love, life and family could be programed into us, just as one of hate, death, and loneliness. It depends on our individual family life. We all need to meditate on that for a moment to see if we can identify any connections between what we saw and what we do.

Let's take a look at school age and being opened up to the world around us. During these years, we are being exposed to others outside of our home and their ways and behaviors. This can be a confusing time as a child. We begin to pick up little habits here and there, according to what we feel we may be able to get away with at home. Confirmation or resentment of dysfunctional practices can set in, depending on how we process things. Our process is based on how our brains operate and the information that has been downloaded into us.

We can see another child's behavior and/or interactions with adults and peers and surmise whether or not that is a behavior that we have seen in our homes. For example, if we are taught not to raise our voices to adults while growing up in an atmosphere that is argumentive, we may not talk back until we see another child doing it. At which point, our little brains connect the dots that expressing verbal outrage *IS* in fact a norm, thereby being acceptable for us as well.

Moving on to Jr high and High school, we begin to see things and behaviors in others a bit more clearly, from a perspective where we are now mature enough to determine what we deem proper and improper. The second time in life that you are the most impressionable is between the ages of 12 and 18, next to the toddler age. We tend to be more compliant from the age of 5 to 11. But that "tween" age group is where independence becomes a reality for us. We need our parents a little less which causes us to believe that we are ready to make firm decisions for ourselves. As skewed a view this may be, it is the first time that we begin to practice critical thinking.

That sense of independence develops, and we are "trying" to find our individuality. Our heart is now open to love and relationships as well. After a few heartbreaks, moving into adulthood, we will have combined those experiences with our experiences growing up, and now we have put in place a "Belief System" of what love truly is to us. If we take those beliefs, and add abuse to them, be it sexual, mental, physical or emotional abuse, we now have a damaged sense of reality, and that damage may become our temporary Identity, i.e. Pain Body. Our Psyche will now be SET on a belief system that may not be healthy, and in some cases, downright toxic to our Being.

In order to deprogram and heal yourself we must first identify, acknowledge, and commit to the process of unlearning and relearning what we think we know.

Fourth Dimension
(Subconscious Database)

The Soul is the Eternal part of Your Being; it is the database that is holding all of our conscious and subconscious memories. This is the part of you that can live in confusion because it is driven by both. Depending on which is dominant and what has been downloaded in us, it can be like a tug of war at times; our Flesh (3D) wants what our Flesh wants, be it money, sex, power, etc.. But at the same time, there is an inner calling from our Spirit (5D), that little voice in our hearts telling us to succeed, but, to do it with integrity; while the big voice in our heads is screaming, By Any Means Necessary. Far too often do we follow the loudest voice, which tends to be the trauma, but we live to regret it later because we know that we've chose what does NOT serve us well. We feel the turning in our stomachs along with the sleepless nights we endure knowing that we may have made a poor decision.

In order to lay that confusion to rest, you must choose which Layer, Spirit (5D) or Flesh (3D), will be the Dominating Force for your life. The Soul feeds and gets its direction through the energy it is fed the most. That is why it is in the center, the (4D) realm.

Our Flesh is vain and self-serving, whereas our Spirit is humble and seeks Righteousness. But, Righteousness is hard to accept in the minds of most. We tend to think it is restrictive and boring, when the truth is, Righteousness is simply doing the "right thing". If you are unsure of what the right thing means, that is where your Spirit (Higher Self) guides. Let me give you a practical example. Let's say that you are walking behind someone and you see them drop an envelope, you pick it up and open it, and see that it has one thousand dollars in it.

Now the Flesh will pick it up and say, "YES this is just what I needed for my bills this month", they may even see it as a blessing, which would be Self-Serving and dishonest. But our Spirit, it will pick it up and return it to its owner, why, because our Spirit thinks outside of self. That one thousand dollars could be the difference between that family being homeless or not. We do not know the troubles that others are experiencing in life, therefore, we should not make decisions and/or judgements as if we do. It is very important that we Be what we Expect of others. That, in essence, is what Righteousness is. The ability to think things through, place yourself in another's shoes, and plant seeds that you do not mind harvesting from.

Your Soul is the one Layer of you that will be paying the price for every decision that has been made for It, your karma. Your Flesh will return to dirt and your Spirit will ascend to The Most High. But your Soul will suffer or prosper depending on how you choose to move.

The "Pain Body" (lowest self) is born at the onset of our first trauma. And we, as human beings stop emotionally growing at that age. So every "negative" experience we have from that point on, is dealt with in the mindset of an eight-year-old, twelve-year-old, etc. etc. And once it is born, it rules our lives, making all the decisions for us and teaching us how to behave and react; all based on the skewed perception that is rationalizes mentally for us. The only way to heal the Pain Body is to reconnect with your Spirit, your Higher Self, your 5D Being.

The Spirit is the "Factory Setting" of us. The part that was created with love, trust, and loyalty, and integrity; before any infusion of anything or any person. Reconnecting to our Etheric

Selves will allow the strength needed to "Get back to the Basics".
The simple life.

Fifth Dimension

(Etheric Being)

Our spirit is the divine part of our trinity. It is that direct connection between Us, the Universe, and our Higher Power. The Spirit is the little voice of warning, correction, and direction we hear when making decisions. Many call it "Intuition"; but it is actually your Divine Self, attempting to guide us to a Higher place of existence. It is what keeps us grounded in Truth and rooted in Integrity. It is the protecting force around us. But let us not confuse your Spirit Being with the Spiritual Realm.

The Spirit Realm is immaterial, sublime, and ethereal. It is the non-tangible space. The Spirit Realm is the space where we made the "soul contract" to enter or reenter this 3D world for a specific purpose. That is where the Architect abides, it doesn't matter what we call it, Universe, God, Spirit, or whatever Deity you choose, it is what we see as a High Power. It dwells in us, formed to animate us, and made to guide us, while we inhabit our somatic state. The "Grand Architect Engineer" of Life. The Creator of all things universally. There is no error or mistake in Its intentions and actions toward us. We made signed a "Soul Contract" with Spirit to accomplish a specific task well before the moment of conception. Our Spirit is eternal and has been in existence for eons. We chose to be here, at this very time and place, for reasons our Natural Being may never remember, but will always gravitate to.

Our spirit is directly connected and unique to us alone. The Spirit Realm is the space in which This Entity exists. There are many spirits in that Realm. Let's explore them.

I am sure you have heard the saying "God is a Gentleman, He does not impose Himself on us, but gives us the power of choice". This is true. We are not forced to live any particular way. We can decide what we deem as suitable for ourselves. However, the Most High has designed a blueprint to give us the best quality of life and the straightest root to our Purpose for being here. What that means is that we can create our future based on our daily Deeds, Thoughts and Words.

All that we have acquired in life, up to this point, has molded who we've become as a Flesh Being.

Both "good" and "evil" abide in the Spirit Realm. Both serving a specific purpose. The "Good" is there to guide us to our purpose and those we are here to touch, and the "Evil" is there to shape and mold our growth as a Spiritual Being. It is there to build our Character and our Faith. Meaning, when there are circumstances that come up in our lives that appears to be tragic or traumatic, those things are used, by the Creator, to teach us a wisdom. Most of us can attest to the fact that we have grown and are stronger because of the things we have endured in this Physical Realm. We tend to reject the lessons because it is too painful. And we forget that the diamonds that are the purest and most valuable are only found deeper you dig into the earth; but they are exposed, clarified, and release their light, through the exposure to the fire.

We have an innate tendency to reach out or look for some "Higher Being" to reconnect with what feels like the missing part of us. Something or Someone to direct us in those unfortunate times. For some of us it is a God, for others it may be Universe. Whatever we identify with, it is a direct longing from our Spirit because our Spirit is aware of that there is "More" than what meets the eye.

So you see, ALL things truly do work together for Good and Purpose. Our Spirit knows our purpose, but until we reconnect with it, we will not be able to see clearly the "Why's" of our experiences.

Reflection:

This is a great moment to stop and think about what your Belief System is today. Ask yourself these questions. Really think them through. Just because we may have been raised under a specific teaching does not mean that it is the path we have to follow. You have a right to choose what works best for you! Spirituality is a very personal thing. The relationship between Your Spirit and Your Source is between the two of you. The question is, do you know and/or stand firm on that choice?

❖ Do you believe in a Higher Power?
❖ Who or what is that being?
❖ In what ways do you acknowledge Your Source?
❖ Do you live by your own belief system or the one you were taught?

Exercise:

- ➢ Just take a moment to evaluate Yourself and see, up to this point, which Layer has been dominating your life, 3D, 4D, or 5D?
- ➢ Acknowledge that Truth and accept it. You have a right to change it if you want to, but you can't change what you don't acknowledge.
- ➢ Spend some time reflecting on what your life experiences have been from childhood through adulthood. Pay close attention to how those experiences have guided you in your decision making. Write them down. Connect the dots. Has your thoughts, feelings, and behaviors been reflecting what you truly believe, or has it been reflective of what you learned.
- ➢ Take inventory on the major good and bad experiences in your life, see how they have enhanced or depleted your Spiritual Being. If you notice that they have guided you more toward being Flesh driven, take a deeper look to find where adjustments can be made.
- ➢ Look from a different perspective, see how strong/weak you are today, how wise or foolish you've been because of those experience. What have you learned and applied to your life because of your trauma?

This should bring you to a place of healing and/or gratitude. When we are able to acknowledge a truth about ourselves, we are empowered to strengthen and to make a change where we see fit. Until we train ourselves to see the light, we will continue to attract darkness. Choose Light!

SUBSEQUENT

LAYER

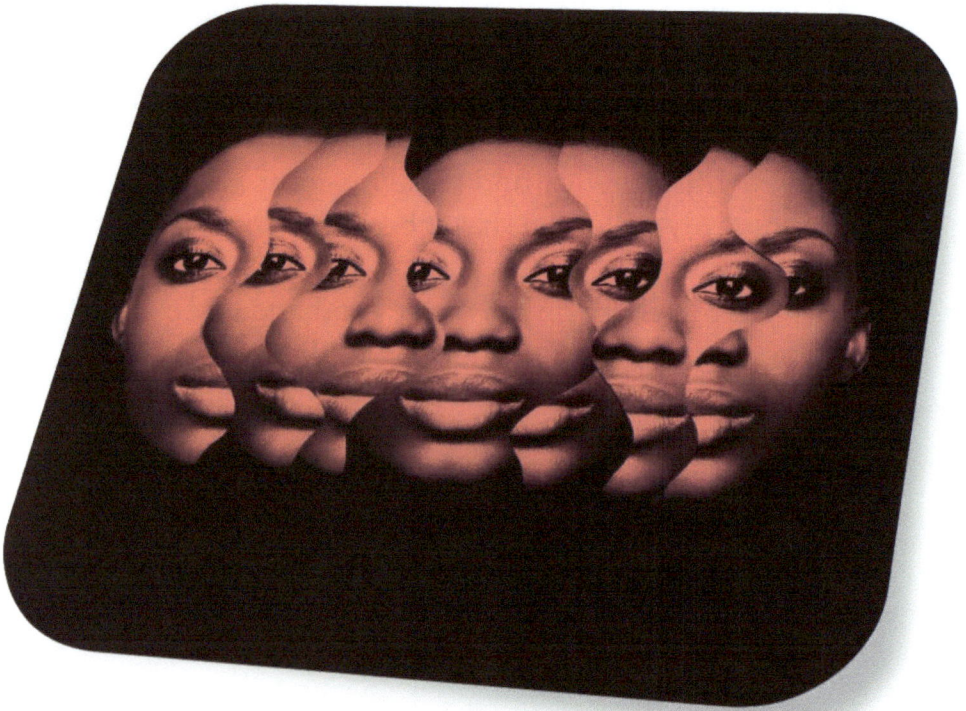

LOVE VS ABUSE

In this section we will dive into the matters of the heart. Women love to love! The question is, are you sure that it is love you are operating in? Love is whole and void of nothing. We are going to explore *Emotional Maturity*, *Love vs Abuse*, *Little Girls Vs Women*, and *Oneness*. There will be exercises woven throughout so that you can take your time and really think deeply as we assess these topics.

Emotional Maturity

Emotional Maturity refers to One's ability to overstand and manage his or her emotions well. As adults, we are put to the test in this area daily. Keeping to the chapter topic of Love, how does Emotional Maturity affect us in our relationships? There are a few signs to look for here. How many of these attributes do you possess?

Are you an insecure lover?

Do you ever find yourself becoming jealous with the presence of, or relationships your partner has with Any woman other than you? For example, saying things to yourself like, He's a mama's boy; No one is that close to their female cousin; Who is the woman at his job staring at me when I stop by; I don't believe guys and girls can be "just friends"? These are just some of the private conversations we have within ourselves when we struggle with insecurity. Sometimes they are not so private conversations when we begin to act out on our thoughts. But keep in mind, unsubstantiated insecurities come from a place deep within. A place that rarely has anything to do with the person you are projecting on to.

If you answered yes to the above question, press pause right here. Think back to the root cause of these feelings, or as I call them, *Lower Emotions.* There has been a moment in time, or moments in time, when you felt unimportant, devalued, invisible, or unworthy. Go back as far as you need to in your memories to find that moment that you began to write the story about you being abandoned and/or rejected.

Insecurities are a symptom, Rejecting or Abandonment are the illness. In most cases, it is contracted through toxic parenting relationships. Especially Daddy/Daughter relationships. A daughter who has had limited access to a father or father figure may not have the tools or proper perspective on how female to male interactions go. They also may not be aware of the way male to female interaction should look. This relationship or lack thereof will impact your relationships to men immensely throughout your life if not addressed and replaced in its perception.

Perhaps you did not get to see healthy, opposite sex, relationships in its pure form as a child. These types of relationships can be very healthy, and very platonic. As the Chief Creations on this planet, there are only two types, Male and Female. We are the perfect balance together. We learn and grow from each other daily and continuously evolve because of each other. It is unrealistic and unhealthy to deprive a human being of human interaction.

But, perhaps you were made to feel inferior as a child or in former relationships; not as pretty as…, not as talented as…, or simply not worthy of happiness. All of these things can leave a person feeling inferior period. And when we feel less than, we become threatened by any woman that crosses our paths that We deem worthy. The fear that your partner, friend, boss, or whoever, will automatically trade you in for the very next person they interact with. And the more confident or evidently well put together that person appears, the stronger your fear becomes.

This is a normal reaction to a traumatized heart. See, as a child, it is our parent's responsibility to build our self-worth. Some of the ways that they do that is by celebrating your development, validating your feelings, showing love through affection and care, reminding you of how beautiful you are, etc. When these things are not taught to us along with all of the other things they are teaching, it causes us to feel overlooked, disappointing, or unimportant. These feelings turn into a tug of war for parental attention and validation. The longer you "go unnoticed", you will then carry that mentality and behavior into adulthood with you and will either become an overachiever and people pleaser or you will completely give up on trying and become emotionless and uncompassionate. Both are two polar ends of the spectrum with no center, in your mind.

Another example could be that you were cheated on by a former lover, or even the one you are with right now? Infidelity is a major blow to one's self esteem. The majority of us automatically look internally to see what we have done or not done to deserve such a betrayal. We have anger towards our partner, but we punish ourselves. That punishment comes in the form of taking on another person's flaws as your fault, owning them, and then applying them to every love decision you make forward.

This behavior is a direct reflection of where we stand with ourselves. Just think about it for a moment; your Spouse/Partner makes a decision to satisfy themselves without regard for your heart or the commitment the two of you have made, and You decide that You are going to take their pleasure and make it your pain. You made up to yourself that their disregard of you was valid and therefore you must now disregard yourself. Not only do you disregard yourself, but you also implement periodic punishments on yourself as well.

That is not to say that betrayal does not hurt and has its place for grievance, but, it is saying that you are owning it as if you were the one who committed the betrayal.

How do we punish ourselves after infidelity? Instead of taking a stand against it and sitting in a quiet place to contemplate whether we choose to forgive and let it go, or if we do not want to be in a relationship with someone who has broken our trust, we tell ourselves that we need to clean up their mess. Not that they need to, but that we need to.

So we begin the process of "bad behavior". We start checking phones, consistently reliving the situation, asking for all kinds of details, and committing all of our time and energy focused on making sure that it doesn't happen again. As if we have the ability to control another person's actions. We throw tantrums and sometimes become violent in our words and actions toward the person. Sometimes they comply and sometimes they rebel, whichever they choose the relationship is damaged and in need of repair. We have now stepped completely out of character and have allowed their pleasure to alter our "SELF"esteem.

When our Self-Esteem has been damaged, it is very hard to stand strong in your worth. Hard, but not impossible. You will forever compare yourself to others if you do not correct it. The key is knowing that you are not directly responsible for the actions of others. Most of us have our own issues as well, and you have to allow them to stay their issues. Your only part in the process is recognizing if you knowingly chose poorly or if you were fooled by a pretender. The best way to exclude the Pretender is by looking at the length of time the relationship lasted. Most people can't pretend for years, at some point the truth of who they are starts to seep out of them. There are a slim few that slip through the cracks, but more than likely we've missed something. For the majority of us, we've just ignored the red flags which means there is something in us that was able to find peace with the pieces we were being offered.

Once you have identified where the negative emotions such as insecurities began, you can begin the healing process.

Keep in mind, that sometimes the script is flipped here, and we are the infidels. We are the ones inflicting the pain on our partners through our actions.

A part of that process is also having a conversation with your partner and/or loved ones that You may have mistreated through your insecurities. Chances are you have left some emotional scars on them from your toxic behaviors. And because they love you, I am sure they will be thrilled to help you in any way possible, because all parties involved can benefit from your growth.

So go ahead, lay down your pride and pick up your Crown. Call up the Queen and do your work!

A Queen is not afraid to admit when she needs support. She knows that there is a nation riding on her back. Her ability to be grounded in her emotions will determine if she rules Affectionately or as Tyrant.

Do you get offended easily?

When people disagree with you or give you constructive criticism, do you find your feelings being hurt right away? Do you become angry or defensive? Do you feel attacked or shamed? Sometimes hurt feelings will show up through tears or anger.

When in a relationship of any kind, one of the primary things we should want, with and for that person, as well as ourselves, is Growth. If when someone's opinion of your interaction or behavior is peacefully expressed, offends you, there is a clear possibility that you are not owning your short comings, or you have not become confident in who you are yet. You could also be relating that opinion to some negative feedback given in your distant or immediate past.

It can be very difficult to hear the hard truth about our self. Especially if you have spent a lifetime being torn down. Sometimes it can feel like another blow. The difference here is that the ones who are speaking to you now, love you, and are attempting to support your growth from toxic behaviors that don't serve you. And when healing from the past has not taken place, it can appear to be more of the same degrading of you.

A widespread mistake I see today in people when choosing who to bring into their lives, is that they do not choose friends and lovers with the view of how we can support each other, and what do we have to add to each other's lives. . We just bring them in. Most times without evaluating the person beforehand. As we are becoming Emotionally Mature we learn that our Energy and Peace are valuable, and we are more careful who we share that with.

As women, we are Receptors; that means that we internalize everything. Many things are planted in us through interaction. The key is to know what things to Digest and what things to Expel. That skill comes with maturity.

When a person has been constantly ridiculed for everything they did or tried to do as a child, teen, young adult, or by a former companion, it makes them defensive, but not in a healthy way to preserve themselves, but in an unhealthy way by building walls around the deception we have told ourselves is true about ourselves. That is a very natural response for someone to have when they believe they are being targeted. But, when we build wall around ourselves we forget that we are isolating ourselves WITH the problems. Leaving us alone to stew in the sess pool of toxic energy.

The real question is, is that what is actually happening today, in this moment? Are you being attacked or are you being enlightened?

Assuming that we have done our best to surround ourselves with loving people who actually care about us, do we truly believe that our loved one's goal is to destroy us; Or is it possible that they are trying to help us grow? The truth tends to hurt, I know, but without it we become stuck in our Pain Bodies, that place where injury resides. As with any injury, if it is not cleaned and prepared to heal, it will not heal properly, and you will periodically feel the results of that injury from that point on. So try to keep an open mind with your inner circle of friends and family. Weigh their intensions with reason.

On the other hand, if the people around us are toxic, and have been draining our energy, it may just be time for a "Life Detox".

You are not obligated to subject yourself to any level of abuse. Be it family, friends, or lovers. You have a right to remove yourself from people, places, and things that bring you pain. Yes, it is true that you cannot choose your family, but you can surely choose how you interact with them.

Life Detox is an issue we will be touching on here in this book, but I will be addressing it more deeply in Layers: Volume II "Finding Balance".

When we are only able to function within dysfunction, that is evidence that we have resigned to a Self-Worthlessness and we make it virtually impossible for peace to find us. So, let's take a minute to identify where we are right now on the "Dysfunctional Scale", and work the process from there.

Think about the last constructive criticism you received from a loved one; did what was said have any truth to it? If you answered yes, Own It! The best way to know this is to actively listen. That means to sit with what is said and process it, weigh it, and see where the truth lies, if anywhere. Then make the necessary adjustments to your hearing and reception so that you can learn and grow versus build more walls that eventually keep only You bound. And until this practice becomes second nature, we must continue to practice it in every situation consciously.

You would be surprised to know how many virulent behaviors we have adopted over the course of our lives. And the fact that we have been using them for so long, we can no longer see their harm. It is referred to as Mental Conditioning.

Mental Conditioning is when you have trained your mind, or your mind has been trained through experience, to react in a certain manner based on triggers. Those triggers govern how we respond.

However, if someone is addressing you in a way that makes you feel inferior and/or disrespected, that is a person you need to have a very firm conversation with about boundaries and verbal abuse. If it continues, you may need to re-evaluate that person's position in your life. ALL of our relationships should be respectful and reciprocal. We should be able to be equally open and honest with those we care about also.

Remember: Love comes to build and never to tear down. Weighing the content of the information you've received, and the heart of the person it came from, before responding, will make a great difference in your perception and growth. Just take one second and Think about what is being said to you. If you do this, you will begin to see that your decision-making process, when choosing whether to take someone's advice or not, will become sharper each time.

Do you feel unheard and/or misunderstood by Everyone?

A common delusion that women have is their belief that people are mind readers; especially men. Women who feel unheard, feel so because They Are! The challenge is finding the Why? Why do we have such a hard time communicating in relationships? Not talking, most women have no shortage there, but actual communication, Solution Oriented Communication now that is the missing link.

The truth is, most of us go unheard because we either have not voiced our feelings at all, or we have not been using the correct language with the person we are speaking to.

Let's explore…

Many women feel misunderstood in their relationships because they speak through their Emotions to get their point across. This is NOT a language many men understand very well. Nor is it a language people who do not care about your feelings understand.

When men see tears, 80% of them do one of two things: They either give in and give you whatever you want, or, they take a leap for cover. They want out of that moment! Out of the conversation and sometimes out of the house and eventually out of the relationship if it persists. The other 20% are an anomaly and are able to sift through and hear the point.

Whichever approach the 80%ers chose, guess what, Nothing has been resolved. They react this way because They Do Not Know What To Do With Your Tears or Your Emotions. It ignites the Protector in him, so he immediately wants to just fix it. Where it becomes a bigger problem for them is if they are the reason we are emotional.

Have you ever noticed how absolutely and wonderfully supportive your guy can be when someone else has upset you? But, let it be him and he suddenly becomes crippled and has no clue how to help you through the pain. It's a stiff pat on the back or an appeasement of sorts. You will see that you get a similar result when screaming at him. He isn't listening to you. He is thinking of ways to get you to shut up quickly or he begins contemplating his exit route. Either way, he cannot hear a word you are saying.

A woman who is operating through her past pains and experiences, tends to use those techniques as a mechanism of control. You want him to react in a way or do a thing that works for you. You want him to "fix it" but Your way. You may win that battle, but you are most certainly losing the war.

Unwarranted tears and a bunch of screaming accomplishes nothing, when attempting to communicate productively. You feel unheard and misunderstood because He is not listening to the problem, he is actively thinking of how to pull a Houdini on you. Active listening requires us to be listening to gain clarity and emotions are never clear.

Ladies, it is imperative that we learn Sound and Productive Communication Skills. That will take effort and discipline on your part. You will have to sit with your feelings for a while and soak it in, process what has happened or what was said, then you have to choose your words carefully and logically. It needs to make sense to him if you want to be understood. Processing your feelings first allows you to speak your truth in no uncertain terms. Speaking from an emotional place is not always productive. It has its time and place.

There are definitely times that we cannot fight back the tears, even after sitting still first, but that is when they are genuine. So go ahead, let them flow. Just be clear that you are in an Emotional State, and may not be thinking clearly enough to bring your point across effectively. But, those processing moments you take before the conversation will definitely bring the crying from hysteria to a pain that he can see clearly.

In those moments, when you are completely overwhelmed by emotions, it is still wise to step back and gather your thoughts before attempting to address the issue; you must take note that Emotions Are Headless. They are all over the place and rarely make sense to anyone. Your ability to Stop, Feel, and Gather your thoughts, then clearly convey what you need to say, even if a change doesn't materialize, you know that you were clear. And now you have to allow them to decide how they want to handle the information they now have.

So, yes, it is true, your feelings of being unheard and misunderstood may be valid. You could be seeing a direct reflection of your inability to communicate well. But that is correctable. The higher your self-esteem is, the better you communicate naturally. It all begins, and ends, with You. We are the ones who train people how to treat us; by how we present ourselves to them and what we tolerate from them.

No one wants to go through life feeling alone and that is what feeling misunderstood or unheard leads to. You can be assertive in your communication without being rude, disrespectful or argumentative. And if you need to cry, get it all out before you have a sit-down conversation. That way if any more tears come up during the conversation you can identify where they come from. There is no time limit to your "time out". Resolution is not a race. Take all the time you need and have the conversation when you are ready.

Sitting with your own feelings and actually feeling them, teaches you what your triggers are. Once you know your triggers, you will get a handle on identifying them and avoiding them until you can transpose them. Now THAT is when you know you have Grown Up in your Emotions.

Recap...

Before communicating, take a step back, calm down, and make your point logically. That may mean you can't address it at that moment. Sometimes not even that day. But, you must make sure that you are level headed, and genuine, before speaking. This technique will be better received by your Partner.

Keep in mind that not all tears are caused by someone else inflicting pain on us. Sometimes, it is the scenario we have created in our own minds that produces them, and sometimes we are remembering something familiar that has nothing to do with the partner we are with, in which case they are not warranted. Nor do they have a place in that conversation. You have to be sure that you are not seeing a behavior and completing its result in your head from some prior place, then making your Partner pay for a mistake they have not made. We must remember that every pot sits on its own bottom. Meaning, no two people are exactly alike. Make your judgements by seeing who is in front of you.

Another double-edged sword that women have, is that our brains are connective. Unlike our counterparts whose brains are compartmentalized. That connectivity is great for our memory, we can see something, and it will remind us of something else. But connectivity is harsh for our trauma for the same reasons. We can identify something in a current relationship that reminds us of something in a former relationship and reenact the response we had then in the Now.

Be Clear…

When people feel spoken to and not spoken at, reception tends to be easier. Just as we tend to make the statements, "I know when he is lying" or "I know my man", well He also knows when you are exaggerating your emotions, He knows his Woman.

Emotional manipulation is a form of abuse and abuse has no place in any relationship.

If you find yourself in any of these examples we have discussed, you have some emotional growing up to do my sister. Are you able to accept that fact, and make the proper steps to improve? Of course you are. You just have to decide to.

> *"The greatest day in your life and mine is when we take total responsibility for our attitudes. That's the day we truly grow up."*

Love vs Abuse

Having a clear understanding, of the difference between Love and Abuse is the key to healthier choices in a Life Partner.

Do you ever feel like you are in the same bad relationship over and over again, just with a different face? That is because we tend to make "Partner Choices" based on Our level of Emotional Maturity. It becomes a vicious cycle of failed relationships. As I said earlier, Love comes to build and not tear down. So can you honestly say that you have truly known Love; or is it what is known as Addiction?

Some of us are "Situationships" and calling them relationships. Having periodic good interactions with someone doesn't mean you are in relationship with them. For example, some of us had periodic good interactions with our fathers and have decided that we have a good relationship with our father. But do you really? When you are in relationship with someone, they don't prance in and out of your life. They don't only show up when it benefits them. You are not optional or convenient, You are a staple in their lives. Anything other than that is a cordial situation.

What is Abuse? Most women don't even realize that they are in abusive relationships, and even less realize that they themselves are the Abusers. "We do not hit each other, so it is not abuse"; that statement is as falsehood and delusional.

Let's take a look into the different types of Abuse as we try to identify if it is present in our relationships.

Physical Abuse:

This one is the most obvious; hitting, pushing, grabbing, choking and so on are easily identified. This behavior is NEVER okay! If you are currently in a relationship like this one, LOVE IS NOT PRESENT, Control Is. A person that uses violence, in any way as to reprimand or correct their Significant Other, sees his/her Partner as a child, or property, not as a Husband/Partner or Wife/Partner.

Men have their own set of issues in terms of Abuse and where it comes from to be dealt with, but this book is for and about Women, so let's not get sidetracked by deflecting.

A woman who accepts such behavior has esteem issues that need immediate attention. She is living to keep her Pain Body alive. Because pain is what she knows, she is in direct alignment with it and attracts it to herself. The pain gives her a sense of normalcy. She is Mentally Conditioned to see Love as painful. There is a void in her so big that no natural thing can fill it. She has to be completely deprogrammed and reprogrammed in order to remove herself from this situation permanently.

My sister, if this is you, take a moment to look back at your life, did you grow up in a household where physical abuse by either of your parents was present; was the abuse toward each other or toward you? Was there a point in time that you felt you were not valuable and was deserving of such behavior? If so, when and what caused those feelings? You must scan your entire life and see where the seed of worthlessness was realized by you. Once you find it, denounce it. Remembering that you were not responsible for another person's pain and or the evil that they took out on you. Give them back their stuff, it does Not belong to you!

However, on the flip side, do you use your hands instead of your words to make your point clear? Do you find yourself hitting, throwing things, shoving, etc., him when he angers or hurts you? If yes, you have to know that your Pain Body has matured to the level of Rage. It could be coming from what you learned at any stage of your life, or it could be that you have so much bottled up pain that it has taken on a personality of its own and shows up to "protect" or "defend" you from whomever or whatever you view as a threat.

You must make some internal adjustments to be able to walk away from an abusive man and/or to stop yourself from being an Abuser. There are many resources out here to help you safely leave or deal with the anger causing the Abuse. Find the root and dig it up. It isn't enough to just pull up the weeds. In some cases, you will need to completely turn over all the soil. This sometimes takes professional support. Do what you need to do to REBUILD YOU, QUEEN!

Mental/Emotional Abuse:

Emotional Abuse is the most common type of Abuse. Yet it is the most overlooked and accepted, almost as a rule in "today's society". Mental Abuse comes through words and actions, but are not physically violent.

Negative words or a betrayal will ultimately drop down into our hearts from our minds, which causes emotional scaring. For example: Your fat; you're ugly; you're stupid; your butt is too big, or your breast are too small, are all ways of attacking one's Self-Esteem negatively. Over time, the abused will cause you to become self-conscious and insecure.

Here's one example of Mental/Emotional Abuse; let's say your Partner has a Proxy. That could be a friend or family member of the same or opposite sex. That person knows all of their secrets, and in some cases, yours too.

Depending on someone for help and support, outside of your partner, is a form of infidelity. So is being the one whom another can depend on more than your Partner can depend on you.

There is a sacred place within a Love Relationship that is reserved for the two of you. No one should be able to reap those benefits on any level. Now, that does not mean that you or your Partner can't receive support from someone else, but what it does mean is that the offered support should not trump or match that which you receive from the one you're committed to.

Even family members can interfere or feel a sense of entitlement in your relationship. Especially those who have known you longer than your partner. And yes, they do have a right to voice some opinions, but once you have committed, especially in marriage, everyone outside of that union has to be put in a place and given an understanding that you are there, and your immediate family (household) has to come first. You have to not just commit to the person you chose, but you also have to trust the person you chose to make good decisions for the life the two of you are working toward.

Being in a relationship is a sacred thing. Cleaving to each other is imperative to keep the bond secure. That is not to say that one should not have outside support and counsel, we all need a support system. I am speaking of the situations where there is very little to no communication within the relationship, because it is all being done outside of the relationship; to the detriment of the relationship.

Another example of this type of Abuse is; Showing attraction for a "type" unlike yours, consistently and blatantly, is Subliminal Mental/Emotional Abuse, which creates an inferiority complex. Some people, both men and women, push the security of their Partner to the limits. This is a breeding ground for insecurity. No one wants to know that every person their Partner is attracted to looks the opposite of them. After a while one will start to question why are you with me, which leads to, "is he/she settling for me", and then that spirals all the way into insecurity and eventually jealousy.

Infidelity, in itself, is a form of Abuse. The betrayal behind the deed can stay with a person for the rest of their lives. If it is never addressed with the person and within ourselves, it will surely cause damage to every relationship forward. That includes interaction with family members and friends. The loss of trust transcends intimate relationships. Because we are connective in our thinking, we do not compartmentalize our trust issues.

For instance, if one of our parents betray us in some way, we generalize it, we even rationalize it. We may say to ourselves, "if my own mother could betray me, anybody can". While that may be true, it isn't expedient. Likewise, when our Partner betrays us, we put their actions on everyone. We don't just stop trusting them, we stop trusting Period.

These behaviors, once they have taken root in our psyche and penetrates our heart, now begin to play and replay over and over for us like a bad movie. At this point, the peace and security within the relationship is altered negatively if not completely lost.

Then there is also the Passive Aggressive manner.

Passive Aggression is when we have a conversation within ourselves and act out the repercussions of those thoughts. But you are the only one who knows the why's for the behavior.

Most women do not realize how powerful our words and actions are for our men. Our men do not require all of the same things we do to feel loved and appreciated. What they do require is to be respected. Speaking down to him, embarrassing him in pubic, placing him behind your friends in priority, allowing other men to do "his job" (i.e. fixing your car, work around the house, a shoulder to cry on), and having an affair may just be the greatest of them all, in terms of disrespect, in the eyes of men. The majority of women cheat with their hearts involved, to a degree. Even if it is just a false satisfaction we receive by having someone to say all the things our man doesn't say anymore. Men know that your heart has been penetrated in some way. In his mind, you have given away a piece of the best part of you. In either case, you have damaged him and your relationship tremendously. These are just some ways in which we as women abuse Mentally or Emotionally.

Evaluate your current and past relationships and see if this abuse has been present. If the answer is yes, you must first correct your thinking and realize that IT IS ABUSE! Next, you need to set new ground rules. Speak up for yourself. Speak up To yourself. Explain to him how those things make you feel. Most times, men equate no complaint as acceptance or approval. If he truly loves you, he will make a conscious decision to discontinue this behavior. But if he doesn't, the control factor is present. And if it is you, the same applies. Just because it has not been address doesn't make it acceptable.

Most men, who abuse in this manner, do it out of an unwillingness to address his own esteem issues. He needs to debilitate you in an effort to not lose you. Now, keep in mind, possession doesn't equate to love. Sometimes, it means he doesn't like being alone and has decided to settle for whomever said yes. You never want to be settled for. You want to be chosen!

If it is you that is the Abuser, follow the same steps. Sit your partner down and talk to him. Get help for yourself, if needed, and if too much damage has been done and the two of you can't fix the relationship, get some couples counseling if it is worth saving.

Sexual Abuse:

Yes, I said it! Did you know that you can be sexually abused while in a relationship? You may ask yourself, how is this possible when I have been sexually active with this man, by choice, all this time? Well let's look at it. Here are some ways that women are enduring sexual abuse without even realizing it.

The one thing that separates friends and lovers is sex. That is an act that is held sacred or should be between the two of you. You can have shared hopes, dreams, thoughts, and feelings with others, but making love is an act reserved for you and your significant other. So when one is sharing that intimate space with another, it can cause a lost feeling within the relationship. A feeling of "what makes me special".

If you are made to feel like an object to him and his friends, and this makes you feel uncomfortable; If you are made to have sex at times that you truly do not want to; If you are made to preform sexual acts that make you feel degraded in any way or are too painful to enjoy; These situations are Sexual Abuse once you have verbalized a clear NO. No one has the right to force you to do or participate in any sexual act or act that is for another's sexual gratification. Sex has to be consensual on all levels.

Did you know that women can sexually abuse their partners as well? We also do all of the things listed above, but the major one we use the most and don't realize it's damaging effects is WITHHOLDING! Yes, yes, yes. Withholding sex from your Partner, as a form of punishment, is Sexual Abuse.

Your partner is an adult in an adult relationship. Punishing him is not your job; Communicating with him is. When you withhold sex from a man you are planting seeds of rejection in him, and that is if they do not already exist, in which case you are watering the toxic seeds. Even more, you are opening him up to his natural instincts as a hunter and conqueror.

My grandmother told me when I got engaged; A good wife makes sure two things are done before her husband leaves out of the front door, his stomach is full, and his nuts are empty. Hahaha! Granny was right. Those two things weigh heavily for a man when choosing a wife. It also weighs in on his ability to maintain his vow of monogamy to you. Many men choose their life partners based on her ability to Nurture, Support and be Nasty. That's not to say that is all a

LAYERS Vol 1: WHO AM I? WHY AM I?

man looks for, but it is a staple that is built on depending on his specific needs. The bottom-line here is be careful ladies. I know we would love to believe that when a Partner cheats sexually that it is their failure alone, but the truth is, we can in some situations aid in that decision being made to do or not to do. Remember, accountability for our actions, or in this case inaction, will help us grow up.

It is not reasonable for us to think that the man we got wild with, made love to almost daily and had a very sexually healthy relationship with, will instantly become a man that no longer need these things as a part of his relationship.

Depriving a man from your intimacy is the equivalent to him depriving you of hugs, kisses, or whatever that "thing" is he has always done to make you feel special. Withholding is a sign of Emotional Immaturity. It is downright Passive Aggressive.

If you can image a five-year-old child who gets mad at their friend or sibling and decides that they are no longer sharing (screaming) "I WANT MY TOYS BACK. THEY ARE MINE. YOU CAN'T PLAY WITH MY TOYS UNTIL YOU SAY SORRY OR PLAY WITH THEM THE WAY I TOLD YOU TO". I know you see how childish, petty, and unproductive it is. We cannot throw tantrums to "get our way". We have to learn to communicate our concerns and be solution oriented in our approach. That is what separates Adults from Children.

Remember, sex in a relationship, is meant to be a physical expression of a couple's love and appreciation for each other. It is mutual and beautiful in its essence. It is the main thing that separates a wife from a friend. It's the one thing that the two of you share only with each other. Whenever one of the Partners begin to allow abuse to creep in,

37 | P a g e

it perverts its actual purpose. A man that truly loves his woman treats her as sacred, she is his Queen, not his property. A woman that truly loves her man treats him with respect, he is her King not her son.

Take a moment to evaluate your sexual relationship with your Partner, and if you see any of these signs of Sexual Abuse, a conversation needs to happen Immediately. If love guides this union, the proper adjustments will be made.

Please understand a few things ladies. Know that your partner is imperfect. He too is the product of his own life's experiences. Some things can be fixed through communication and/or counseling and some cannot. It is up to you to find that out. It is up to you to know your threshold of tolerance with full awareness that he too has a threshold.

Financial Abuse:

This particular form of Abuse is felt but not identified as Abuse. Mostly because we live in a society that prides itself on independence. Men have to be providers and women have to also be able to provide for themselves. Where the abuse comes in is where the two have become one and one of the two deprives the other of basic needs and/or the lifestyle they have become accustomed to, based on their "ill behavior". These behaviors can cause a Partner to step outside of the Union for support or even make consequential decisions to make life more comfortable.

When you decide to share life with someone, finances need to be very clear as to how they will be managed. And BOTH parties need to adhere to the guidelines set in place. Withholding basic needs and/or choosing to take from the family to satisfy personal desires, i.e. gambling, shopping addictions, spending money on affairs, etc. These are all forms of financial abuse and can surely lead to the breakdown of any relationship.

I will leave this section with one last exercise.

Evaluate Self! Men are not the only ones who Abuse, women do too. If you are the Abuser in your relationship, you MUST stop! Get help if you need to. Just know that true love does not include Abuse.

"One's dignity may be assaulted, vandalized and cruelly mocked, but it can never be taken away unless it is surrendered."

Michael J. Fox

Girls' vs Women

The "Ah Ha" moment. Who makes the decisions for you? Life can be cruel at times, I know. And most women have suffered some sort of Abuse before adulthood. Studies show that once abuse has taken place our Emotional Development is arrested. At that moment we develop our "Pain Body". The Pain Body is subconscious, it has great power and momentum to develop patterns in our lives that lead us to Self-Sabotage.

The Pain Body is the little girl that lives deep within, that has endured trauma on an emotional and/or physical level. She now builds a fort around herself only allowing pain in and only putting pain out. How do you know if you are operating as that Little Girl through the Pain Body she has created, or if you are operating with Emotional Maturity as a Grown Woman?

Well first, if you found yourself identifying with the toxic behaviors we've spoken about thus far, chances are you have a Little Girl running your Adult Life. As odd as it may sound, it is very common. We all have an inner child, that child, when healthy, is what allows us to love, trust and give purely. She not only sees good, but she is good.

Children under the age of about four, have no long-term memory settings yet. That means that they can experience some bad things (not necessarily traumatic), but not so good things, and still maintain the Purity of Heart. They will continue to trust as if nothing has happened. Adulthood is what teaches us the lessons of using wisdom.

But when one's inner child has experienced a multitude of traumas, it will find ways to secure itself against further trauma. This is where the childlike behaviors begin because we have not dealt with the pain nor have we learned any techniques to handle conflict when it arises as we get older.

The Grown Woman

She is grateful for all that she has earned and acquired. She sees her Partner clearly. She understands not only his flaws but also his efforts and is able to acknowledge them. She holds him in high regard and expects the best from him. But her expectations are not of the kind that decides how he should operate, but the kind that he will always be the best Him that he can be. Therefore, she does not read his every action or request as a reason to fight. She knows her man and his heart, because she is healed from her pain body and feels no need to control him. She is able to make sound judgements. She picks and chooses her battles carefully. She would rather be Happy than Right all the time. She also realizes that she has imperfections as well, so she does not hold her man to unrealistic standards, that she herself, could never live up to. In other words, she leaves room for error within the relationship and is committed to working together to grow and evolve as a unit.

The Little Girl

Her actions are reactions nothing short of tantrums. They are counterproductive and makes her Partner feel unappreciated, and devalued. In turn, it will begin, over time, to drive a wedge between the two of them. The little girl is controlling. She needs to feel she can intercept more pain from entering her life. While in actuality, she is preparing a place for more. She is loud and unreasonable. She cannot see past her own wants and needs. She is very self-serving because she refuses to go without Anything again. The Little Girl does not see her own flaws authentically, and the ones she does see, she counts as a byproduct of her hard life. She takes very little responsibility for her actions. She sees other men in every action that her man takes. That other men she sees are generally her past Abusers.

Here are some examples of challenges, in a relationship, and how we react to those challenges. Take a self-inventory to see where you may fall?

"Challenge"	Little Girls	Grown Women
He purchased you both a gym membership today	*Hurt or angry* So you think I'm fat?	*Excitement* We have been talking about a healthier lifestyle for years.
He cleaned the kitchen before you got home from work	*Ungrateful* You didn't even sweep/mop the floor.	*Appreciative* So glad I only have to do the floors, I am so tired today.
He gave the kids a bath and put them to bed before you got in	*Frustration* Ugg, now I have to clean up all the water everywhere.	*Supportive* Lights some candles and prepare an intimate evening.
He bought you an engagement ring	*Embarrassed* This diamond is so small. You are cheap.	*Valued* He thinks enough of me to make me his Wife.
He works 60 hours a week	*Rejected* You never spend any time with me.	*Focused* What can I be doing to help out, so he can be home more?
He treats his mother like a Queen	*Jealous* He is such a mama's boy; I wish he would just grow up.	*Understanding* So that's why he is so good to me. Their relationship is awesome.
He wants a guy's night out	*Insecure* Why, so you can be out there checking out other women? When do I get a day off?	*Relieved* I love having a chance to miss him, and I get some me time as well. WIN WIN!
He requests "wind down" time after work	*Selfish* For what? You've been gone all day. I need a break too.	*Supportive* Maybe he had a rough day today. Let me prep the kids for bed.

Little Girl behavior can also be weak or passive. In this instance, her responses to every request or demand is an automatic Yes. She is afraid to speak up for herself out of fear of losing the relationship. No matter how much a thing is killing her on the inside, she will go along with any and everything to keep the peace. This is unhealthy behavior, and a tell tell sign of Emotional Immaturity, usually stemming from fear of being alone or failure. Both are examples of Low Self-Esteem. There is a fine line between Submission and Subservience.

Submission is a choice and is made based on love and respect; whereas Subservience is an obligation based on fear and duty. Grown Women are able to make a decision to submit "with" her partner, based on what she feels best serves her life. Little Girls see submission as taking an inferior roll in the relationship thereby being unable to do it out of fear that she will not have the control she needs to protect herself. So she will either be a tyrant or a subservient in her relationship, depending on the nature of her abuse and how it relates to her personality.

Reflection:

The "Damsels in Distress" only attract men that need to fix someone to feel empowered. This is the definition of a Co-dependent relationship. We only attract what we are, or where we are. So, attracting a controlling or abusive man is a direct sign that there is a little girl trapped in a grown woman's body seeking validation of our "Pain Body" vs Elevating to the next level. What that means, in its truth, is that you are currently emotionally immature and out of alignment with your Spiritual Self, your Higher Self.

Exercise:

Take a thorough look into your relationship, and see if you are damaging it through your pain body. Think about the man you have chosen, and his actions, rather than your assumptions. Recall the last argument you had, what could you have done differently? Did you over react? Was his point or request valid or reasonable? What were your reactions and words to him? Did they build or tear down?

If your answers to these questions lead to a bunch of yeses, you are currently in an adult relationship as a child. It is time to GROW UP YOUR EMOTIONS! The path to doing so is to first identify where you stopped growing. When was your pain body born? Once you know this, you can begin to deal with your pain and heal yourself and your relationship.

You will need to then begin helping him to heal from the damage you have caused him. Rebuild your King through acknowledgment, acceptance and change of all those toxic behaviors. Sit him down and talk to him. Tell him your truth and what the plan is to fix it. Apologize sincerely. Work your plan!

Oneness

What exactly is *Oneness*? The definition of Oneness is the Fact or State of Being Unified or Whole, through the compromise of two or more parts. So, let me pose a question. Are you and your partner living this definition of Oneness?

Let us take a practical view of what Oneness looks like...

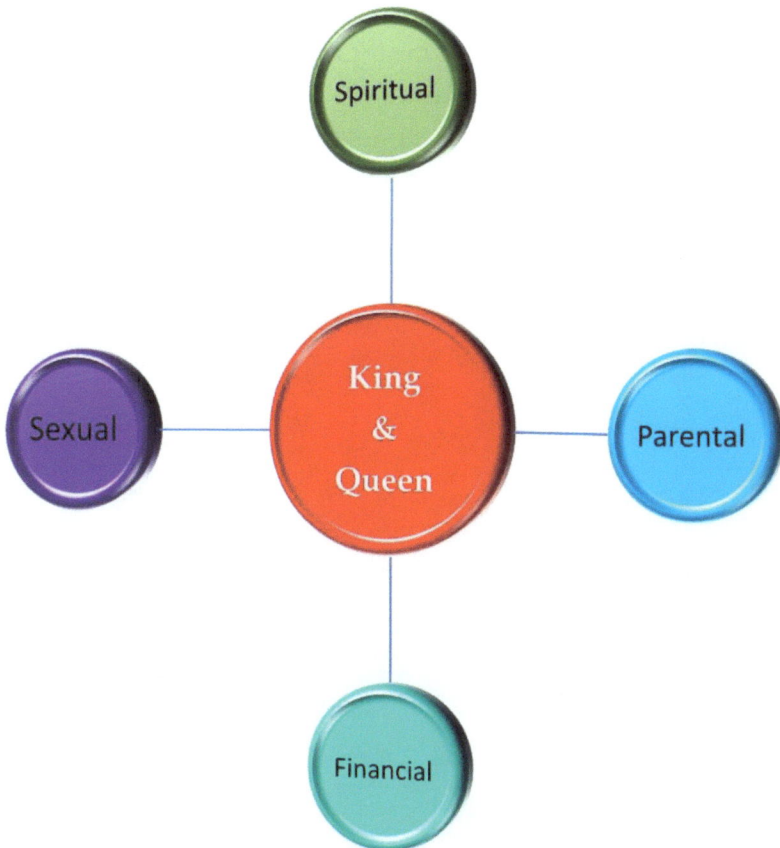

Every relationship has to stand unified in these Four Major Components for it to become ONENESS. They are literally the load baring walls in a relationship. The structure can stand long without load baring walls; it won't withstand the storms. However, it is the Interconnecting Rings that not only connect those walls, but they are also the shield that protects the Unit from infiltration, while leaving room for the Unit to continue to grow and expand, together. The only way to penetrate the Unit is for one of or both of "The ONE", places tears in those Connectors, in which case, others can sneak in or be snuck in.

Without an agreement being reached in any of these areas, there will inevitably be a breakdown in the relationship. Once the circle is broken, the King and Queen are now exposed to outside forces. Let's look at them one at a time, and break them down for clear understanding.

Spiritual

A person's Spiritual Belief System is the driving force for most of what they do, and what they won't do. It even tends to govern the principals they live their entire lives by, when they are active in their Belief System. And it is very hard for certain Spiritual backgrounds to actually cohabitate.

Our Spiritual Belief System is the only one, of the four components, that can cause the entire Unit to collapse. For example, if I am a devout Christian Woman, who has taken Jesus Christ as her Lord and Savior, living by standards of the Holy Bible, but my Partner was raised an Atheist, believing that no "God" exist, we are going to have problems in every area of our relationship. Let me show you using our example couple.

The Christian Woman is going to want to build her household on Christian doctrine. Meaning, raising her children in her faith (Parental). She is also going to have a desire to pay tithes and offerings to her church (Financial). Finally, she will take a biblical approach to sex with her Partner (Sexual). Now for that Atheist Man, he will not be on board with any of the above, due to his own feelings concerning Religion. This is the beginning of division. Which stacks the odds against you very early on if you discuss it, and an even more contentious situation if you wait and discuss it later into the relationship.

When we are in the dating stages of a relationship, especially in the beginning, we tend to steer clear of controversial conversations. Most times we are so wrapped up in the "New Love" feeling and do not want to disturb that. So religion and/or faith doesn't really come up in any detailed way.

But, once the relationship progresses, it comes up here and there. We convince ourselves that it's a small thing and that we will be able to work through it. The majority of our focus is on the "big issues". If we don't see any signs of former abuse and/or bad relationship concerns, we keep moving forward. Ultimately negating the fact that we are considering spending the rest of our lives with this person and any cracks in that foundation has the ability to spread and eventually crumble.

Be sure that you cover this topic early on in the dating process. The last thing you want is to find out after marriage or children that your Partner worships potato chips and wants to raise your children to do the same. ☺

Parental

This is a topic that most couples do not discuss in detail before marriage or having a child together. I am not sure why that is, when Parenting is the most powerful contribution one can make to this earth. We do ourselves, and our Partner, a disservice by Not having this conversation. Some people see it as a deterrent if you talk about children too soon, but I say If you see this person as a real candidate for your love, you have to.

Some of the questions we should explore with someone prior to relationship are…

1. Do you have/want children?
2. How is your relationship with the child(ren)'s mother(s)? (this speaks to his values as a man)
3. How often are they with you? (speaks to his involvement as a father)
4. How many children, or how many more children do you want?

5.   What are your opinions on discipline and education for your children? (there must be agreement here)

6.   Have you ever been accused of and/or convicted of ANY TYPE of child abuse? (I suggest that couples do a background check for this one together. We live in an outrageous world today and most children suffer sexual abuse by family members.)

Now I can almost guarantee that your mouth dropped at number 6. Well answer me this, would you rather know before or after you bring him around your children, or have one with him, that he is a pedophile or aggressively beats children? I'll let you think that one through while we move on.

Financial

Money is a major cause for divorce in this day and age. When couples don't agree on how they view and spend money, they are bound to run into issues. For example, there are two types of mindsets when it comes to money, the Saver and the Spender.

The Saver

The Saver is one who always has future responsibilities in mind; college funds, rainy day accounts, investments, and vacations, which are all very important to a family's future as well as their quality of life. They tend to be frugal, always looking for the best deals on everything.

The benefits of a Saver are that they tend to be more responsible and have a clear overstanding of what money is. The whole family benefits from this.

The drawbacks of the Saver are their inability to live in the moment, and enjoy life as it comes. They don't realize that they cannot take it with them when they part from this earth. Someone will enjoy life for them, with all of their stored-up money, if they don't live a little.

The Spender

The Spender is one who has already figured out what to spend the money on, before they even get paid. They tend to be quite a bit more frivolous than the Saver. This person lives paycheck to paycheck generally; weekend activities, that new outfit or pair of shoes, loans to family members or friends, are priorities.

The benefits of being a Spender is the ability to be spontaneous, which is great for relationships.

The drawback is the irresponsibility factor. Spenders tend to put fun and Image before responsibility which can cause the family to struggle more than they have to.

Both of these types are needed in the relationship for there to be balance. It is important to identify Who is Who early on. You can get your first glimpse in the dating phase by just observing your potential partner. Once the relationship looks as if it has the potential of getting serious, a financial conversation needs to happen. Not once you are IN the relationship.

I never recommend like-mindsets to date each other. It only leads to poverty or redundancy. Either would raise challenges for the couple at some point during the relationship. The key to making it work is respect and understanding.

The Spender must allow the saver to handle responsibilities first. Adjust the spending to the family budget. Likewise, the

Saver must also leave room for excitement and spontaneity. It is important that relationships are not completely predictable. Balance is key. Allow your partner to indulge a little. It will keep that flare that every relationship needs. The future is important but not promised. Your present is what you have for sure. Embrace it, with one eye on tomorrow, just in case you are blessed to see it.

Sexual

This is a touchy topic in the dating phase if you have not been intimate yet. Especially if you don't want to come off as a hypersexual, but there are some things that are important to know before committing yourself. I would much rather know walking into the bedroom rather than learn it there. That could be a mood killer.

For instance, what type of sex drive does he have? What is he "in to"? What are his "No" zones? Does he know mine? Is he free of all diseases?

Sexual Compatibility is very important. Exploration is good, but most of us have a fine line drawn in the sand; even the freest minds.

Let's look at each one and see how it can affect your relationship negatively or positively.

- *What type of sex drive does he have?*
  Imagine committing to a man that is impotent or only wants sex twice a week, but you are at your peak and need it daily if not more. Ultimately you will find yourself being

dissatisfied with your Partner and a Pain Body will kick in through the feeling of rejection. And those "connectors" begin to weaken you by way of your self-esteem and/or self-worth.

That applies to you both. If he is hypersexual and needs sex all the time and you don't, the same challenges will be there. You need to know these things so that the proper compromise can be reached, if you feel the relationship is worth it.

- *What is he in to?*

You need to be clear in this area prior to engaging your heart. Even his fantasies are necessary information to keep yourself from falling into a sexually abusive relationship. If your man is heavily into porn or S&M (sadism & masochism) you need to know. If he believes that sex is only for procreation, you need to know that too. If you are not open to his liberal side, or even his conservative side, you will be ultimately dissatisfied with him as a partner. And dissatisfaction leaves room for poor decisions like infidelity.

- *What are his "No" zones?*

This information is imperative. A woman can take a man from 100 to 0 in 2.5 seconds flat by just touching the wrong spot. It is just as important for you to know what he is comfortable with as it is for him to know what you are comfortable with. "No" zones not being discussed can be dangerous. For anyone to be touched and/or penetrated in a place that is uncomfortable can destabilize the relationship and create trust issues. Have the conversation!

- *When was his last STD and HIV test?*

I am a firm believer in exchanging paperwork on this, prior to having sex. Not because either of you are deceptive in any way, but because many Sexually Transmitted Diseases can lay dormant for years without any signs or symptoms. Especially in men. That applies to HIV as well. Get tested! You can do it together. But always use protection. My recommendation is that you go through 2 cycles of testing six months apart before even thinking about removing the condom.

However, as adults, we know that there comes a time in every relationship when the protection either leaves all together or we have that "oops" moment. Better safe than sorry. So exchange those papers beforehand.

Your bottom-line here is Communication. You can keep your circle tight and maintain the Oneness between the two of you by talking about the tough stuff before the commitment. Proactivity is better than Reactivity. One grants peace and the other anxiety. Which do you prefer?

TERTIARY

LAYER

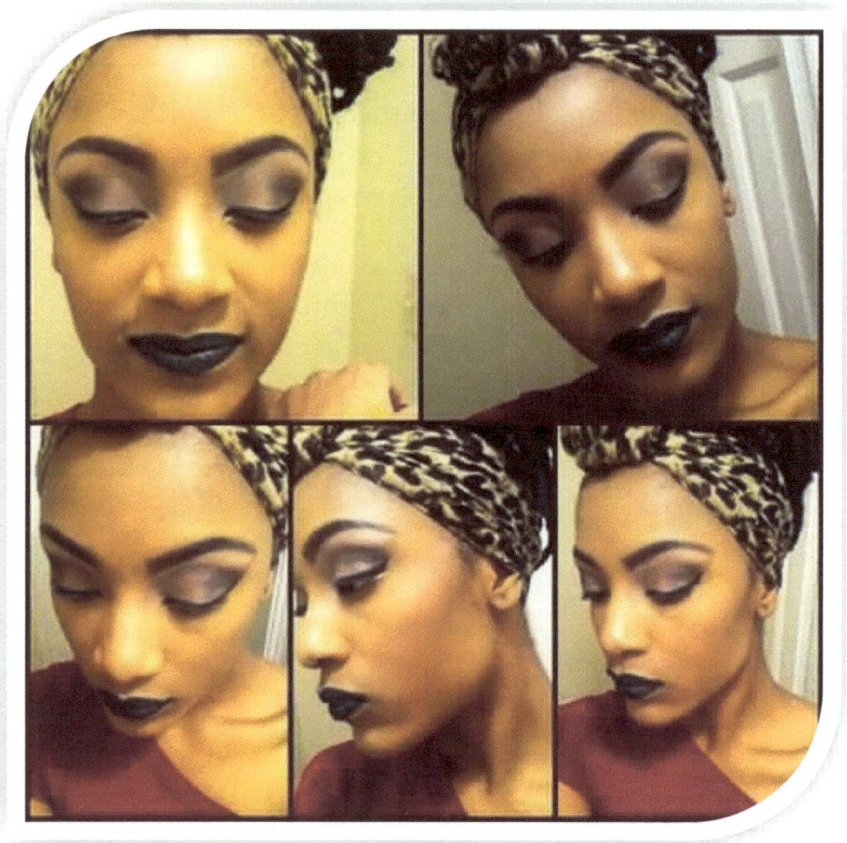

LETTING GO

Well my Sisters, we made it through the hardest parts of the process, Self-Realization. It is overstood that when we have to take a critical look internally, it can leave us feeling a little bummed, but do not worry, here is where we begin to put all the pieces back together in a healthier manner.

If we do not identify our True Selves and what lies beneath the surface, we cannot make any adjustments. And we become destined to repeat the toxic cycle that we've been in.

Take a moment to look back on all of your exercises, notes, and the Evaluation Test you took at the beginning of this book.

Once you have compiled a grand picture of who your "authentic self" is, stand still and own it. Own it, because it may very well be the last time you will ever have to see her. It is time to detach from your Pain Body and allow the Woman, the Queen, to evolve and guide your future.

The concept of Letting Go, is a cutting of the cords that bind you; be it abuse, low self-esteem, poverty, and so on. In order for your Divine Being to emerge out of this bondage, you have to begin to make some different decisions for your life, wouldn't you agree?

You already know how the story ends if you choose to continuously repeat the same behaviors over and over again, your today will become your forever. You know that book very well and have read it a million times before. And the fact that you have chosen this book to read, tell me that you are sick and tired of that story.

If you are ready, let us start with some simple yet powerful exercises.

We must first reprogram the subconscious to impact the conscious. The two of them are connected with the subconscious being the more powerful of the two.

Our conscious minds give us room to make changes in the moment. Our subconscious minds guide our behaviors through the conscious mind without evident reasoning. It remembers everything that we have buried, so by tackling it, through deliberate reprogramming, we gain control of our minds, as a whole, giving us the power over our entire selves. It is virtually impossible for us to heal what we don't identify.

Calling up our pain is a daunting task, but an absolutely necessary.

Here are some practical ways to put the past behind you and lay that Pain Body to rest once and for all.

...And Then She Exhaled

<u>Five Steps to Recovery</u>

Exercise 1: Forgiveness

We live in nothing short of a sick world today. There are so many damaged people continuing the cycle of damaging others. If you decided to purchase this book, that most likely means, you have encountered some of them yourself. If you made it this far, through the book, you are ready for change. I am so proud of you! Now it is time to truly LET GO!

This exercise may be the most difficult of them all. But I promise you, if you can make it through it Effectively and in Truthfully, you can finally be FREE.

Make a list of every person you can think of that has ever hurt you in a life altering way, be it through their actions (abuser) or inaction (absentee parent), write them all down in list form. Next you are going to number the list by pain level (i.e. 1 being the most impact and 10 being the least). Once your list is complete, you will write a letter to each individual starting with the least impact.

Now don't worry, I am not going to ask you to give it to them. This is for you. Be as detailed as you can in your letters. What happened? How did you feel in that moment? In what regard did you hold that person, prior to the incident? What did you feel towards them right after? How do you feel their actions impacted your life most? What do you feel for that person today as you stand? This portion of the book may take a few days. Give yourself all the time you need.

Once your final letter has been written, grab a cup of tea or a glass of wine, whatever your preference. Sit back and read them out loud, one by one. Allow the tears to fall, the anger to come up, or whatever emotion you feel. Remembering that It Wasn't Your Fault. You are not responsible for another person's pain or dysfunction. And the fact that they chose you to take it out on doesn't make it yours to carry. So get it all out, because this is a funeral service for your Pain Body. And You will be giving the Eulogy.

Feel free to share this moment with your Partner, or best friend, if you feel you need support. Once the emotional stage has past, it is time to prepare for burial. Whether you choose to bury or cremate the letters (the trauma) is your choice, but I recommend cremation because none of those memories deserve to exist anymore. Nor does their effects.

Sometimes it can be hard to let go of something that has been a part of you for what seems like forever, but the time has come. You have to accept the apology you never received and forgive. Forgiving is not excusing, it is a purging of the soul's memory of the pain and residue that the act caused. This forgiveness is for You! You must recite these words right before doing either.

Repeat after me...

"Today I CHOOSE to forgive everyone that have wronged me in my lifetime. Today I CHOOSE to forgive myself for blaming myself for things that were out of my control. Today I CHOOSE to no longer live my life as a victim. Today I CHOOSE to let yesterday die as yesterday has. These letters represent my Toxic Layers. Out of those Layers my pain was born, and along with these letters my pain will be no more.

I release myself from the aftermath of these experiences. I commit myself to live the life intended for me by my Creator.

TODAY (state date) I (state name) AM NO LONGER LIVING THROUGH TOXIC LAYERS! I AM WHOLE!"

Now lay your Pain Layers to rest!

Exercise 2: Humility

Reconnect with your Higher Being. No matter what your faith is, there is always a Governing Source. Pray More! Meditate More! Choose your "Personal Path" and walk it out Every Day. Having a Spiritual Awareness helps us to not be so self-absorbed. It also puts things in perspective for us. Acknowledging that there is a Higher Power gives a sense of security, establishes moral values, and an "Ultimate Goal" to look forward to and work towards. Return to your "original state", your Divine Self. When we are born, we are Pure, that is when we are the closest to the likeliness of Our Creator. Reconnecting will reestablish this for us. And allow us to allow our ashes to become our beauty.

Exercise 3: Humanity

Give Alms. Giving Alms is simply an act of kindness towards those less fortunate than you. It can be in the form of money, food, or even donations (clothes, shoes, anything in good condition you no longer have use for).

For example, the single mother down the street who is evidently struggling. You could pick up a few extra things while grocery shopping, give her clothes for the children your family can't use or don't wear (good condition of course), or if you are in the financial position, offer to help out with a bill. You get the idea. We reap what we sow. If you sow seeds of love and kindness, that becomes the harvest you reap.

We only get out of this life what we put into it. Karma is the return on your investment, be that what it may. You have the power to dictate what Karma will bring to your life. The "Law of Attraction" is real. What we put out into the atmosphere comes full circle; even if it doesn't come back from the specific ground in which we sowed it. This is called the "Circle of Life".

Exercise 4: Positive Affirmations

Take a moment to grab some multi-colored sticky notes. You are going to write these five affirmations on them (one per sheet). Then place them in the five places listed and read them aloud EVERYTIME you encounter one.

1.   I am bold, I am beautiful, and I am powerful! I am the Author of my Fate. Today I will plant good seeds into my life and will not allow anything less from this world! (Bathroom mirror)

2.   Someone woke up and will return to sleep on the street today. Someone may not be able to eat today. I am grateful for every blessing in my life. (Bedside)

3.   My body is a Temple, what I put in it DOES MATTER! I choose my health. (Refrigerator door)

4.   Today I may run into the CEO of that company I want to work for, or my Future Husband. What first impression do I want to portray? (Closet door)

5.   TODAY IS GOING TO BE A GOOD DAY! Nothing will come up that I cannot handle gracefully. (Front door)

Now the key is to change the paper color once a week but not the message. By doing so, we hope to accomplish two things. First, rewriting them will commit them to memory over time. Eventually you will find yourself speaking them out without reading. Second, by rewriting them they will not become a simple piece of your décor only to be ignored with time.

Exercise 5: Self-Love

Make these three commitments to yourself. You matter too. You are valuable. It is imperative that you know and accept this fact. Before you can fall in love with anyone, you must first Fall in love with You!

1.   *Date night* – Take yourself out on a date once a month. Just you! It could be to dinner, a movie, the park, etc. In order to fall in love with someone, you must spend time with them. Get to the place where you love your Own company and everyone else will follow.

2.   *Take a Break* – Commit to taking two 15-minute breaks every day. Doing this will keep you on track. Just stepping away sometimes and breathing can do wonders for your psyche. Give your mind a rest, You deserve it!

3.   *Become a Writer* – Start keeping, what I call, a Growth Journal. A growth journal allows you to record your progress. Your Growth Journal allows you to keep an account of all of your successes and challenges along the way.

At the end of the day, recount the day in your journal, and jot down those moments you were really proud of. It could be how you handled a stressful situation, or a great meal you cooked, it could even be a complement you received on the NEW YOU!

You also want to start an Anger journal. This will allow you to record your less positive experiences in a different space. That way you can keep your successes and challenges separate. By doing this you will have a record of how effectively you are using the new tools you've acquired.

In your anger journal, this is where you go when you have to take those steps back to process before reacting. It is also a place for you to release your negative emotions so that you are not starting a new "basket of disappointment" in your subconscious. Remember how much it took to empty the one you once had.

The anger journal is not a place to revisit (reread), that is not the goal. The goal is to have a tangible way to see how many more good days you are having than bad. Being able to recognize how many more times you pull out your Success Journal vs your Anger Journal shows continued improvement and growth.

Now your success journal can be your "go to" when you are feeling discouraged or overwhelmed. A reminder of how far you have come. A biography of how truly amazing you are and how productive your life has become. All of those entries will remind you of why you can't give up.

Never give up! You got this Queen!

CROWN

RESTORED

Empress Order

AFTERWORD

YOU DID IT! You should feel a sense of Pride and Accomplishment.

My sisters, we all have been the Little Girl in this book at some point. The only difference is, to what degree for each of us. And with all that has been revealed during this process, I hope you were able to see what I saw as I walked it through before even writing this book. I had to look in the mirror one day and say "Makeda, you are crazy, and you HAVE to do better". That statement wasn't about me belittling myself, it was about Owning the state I was in in that very moment; and vowing to do something about it.

For me the hardest part was writing the letters to my abusers and those by whom I felt abandoned. That took me a couple of weeks. Simply because my process was to first remember it completely, feel the anger, then the pain, then my pen would move. And I couldn't handle facing them all in one day. So I took my time starting with the simplest one and working my way down the list to the hardest. Funny thing is as I was working my way through my list, I started to see where I was holding anger toward people that I held responsible for Not knowing what I didn't tell them. That was eye opening. I realized that those letters needed to be apology letters, so that is what I did.

Every one of us will have a different experience with this process and will learn different things about themselves. You'll meet the little girl deep inside from your yesterday, as well as the pain body who had become your "Ride or Die". Don't be ashamed of what you find. Always look for the origin of it and replace the memory of that trauma with the strength you found through it. That is what I call transposing. For example, if you have been physically abused by a partner, after you release responsibility from yourself for the actions they committed and give them back their stuff, you can then replace the memory of that abuse with the new information you have to identify the signs of abuse well before having to experience it. You are now an Expert and a graduate of the "school of hard knocks". You now have something of value to offer your sister.

As for working toward Emotional Maturity, that is an unending process. Life will always test this part of you. After all, we are women and emotions are a part of our makeup. So as odd as it may sound, I consider myself a "Recovering Dysfunction Addict". Because I believe that there are still moments that I turn into a big brat or a tyrant to make a point. But I have those episodes less and less now. I am extremely cognitive of my triggers, as well as People, Places, and Things I need to stay away from. This will be you as well. Never think that healing means that you will never be challenged again.

Just keep in mind that the Pain Body had become like a huge tumor crushing your vital organs, and so it had to be surgically removed to save your life. Nothing could work properly as long as it was there. But, that means there is a healing process that you have to endure next. Don't make any sudden moves. Take your time and heal. You will see once it is all said and done, that you are moving much better

Thank you for your support! If you know a sister that could benefit from the tools in this book, please gift her a copy. As women, we must have a common goal, which is The Healing of a Nation. Remember it all begins with Us. We are the Child Bearers and the first Teachers of every new Human Being on this earth. Let us heal ourselves first. So that we can execute some damage control out here in this world.

WE ARE POWERFUL!

WE ARE BEAUTIFUL!

WE *ARE* THE

ORIGINAL

QUEENS!

Peace & Blessings!

ALSO AVAILABLE....

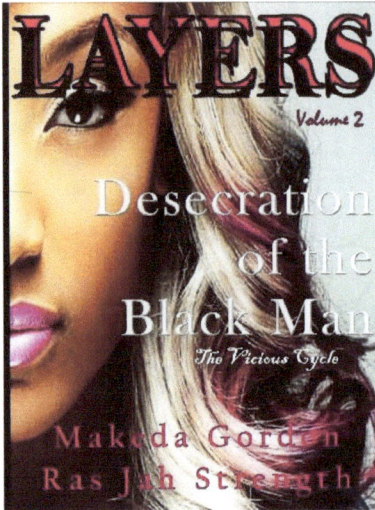

Layers Vol. 2
Desecration of the Black
Man
"The Vicious Cycle"
The Black Woman is the
Strength of the Black Man. She
is his Light. But, sometimes
we don't realize our own
Power.

Layers Vol. 3:
Lord… Why Am I Not
Married? Because You're Not
Single!
We often get caught up in the
"idea" of being married, but most
do not realize what it is they are
truly asking for. You can't Master
Marriage until you Master Single!

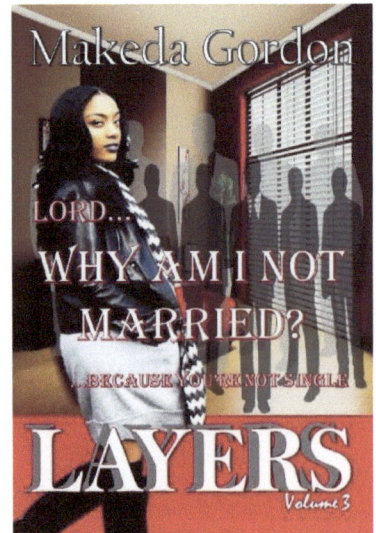

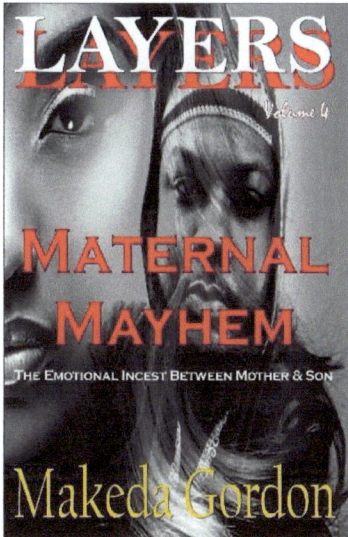

Layers Vol. 4: Maternal Mayhem

What type of Mother are you? In what ways could you be hurting their development vs supporting it? Let's find the challenges so that we can fix it.

Layers Vol. 5: Finding Balance After Healing

The ability to balance out your life requires a total Alignment. We are not One-dimensional beings. It is our Layers that make us who we are. Learning to listen to your inner voice, Your Divine Self, will place you on the path to finding the balance you need to have a peaceful life.

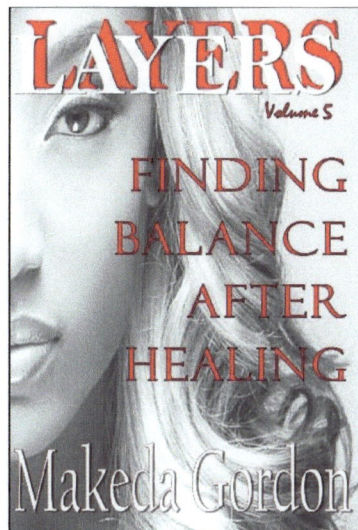

Layers Vol. 6: Empress Order

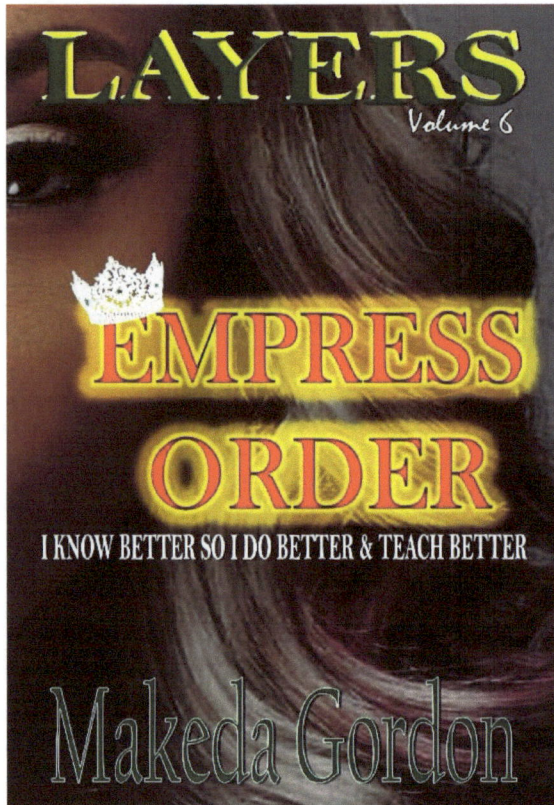

To operate in *Empress Order*, you must create your life and environment. An Empress does not adapt to her surroundings, She causes her surroundings to adapt to her. She does not give away her power; She does not compromise her moral fiber. She lives out loud. She walks in Truth and Light. She is an example of what a Woman is.

For more about Solomon & Makeda Publishing, or to make a purchase, visit us at www.sm4publishing.com

For more about One-on-One Coaching with Empress Order, or to make a purchase, visit us at www.empressorder.com

To Schedule an Empress Order Seminar:
theitalempress@gmail.com

Social Media:

Facebook @empressorder

Instagram @empressorder

www.ingramcontent.com/pod-product-compliance
Lightning Source LLC
Chambersburg PA
CBHW051234090426
42740CB00001B/17